This Little Princess
story belongs to

· · · · · · · · · · · · · · · · ·

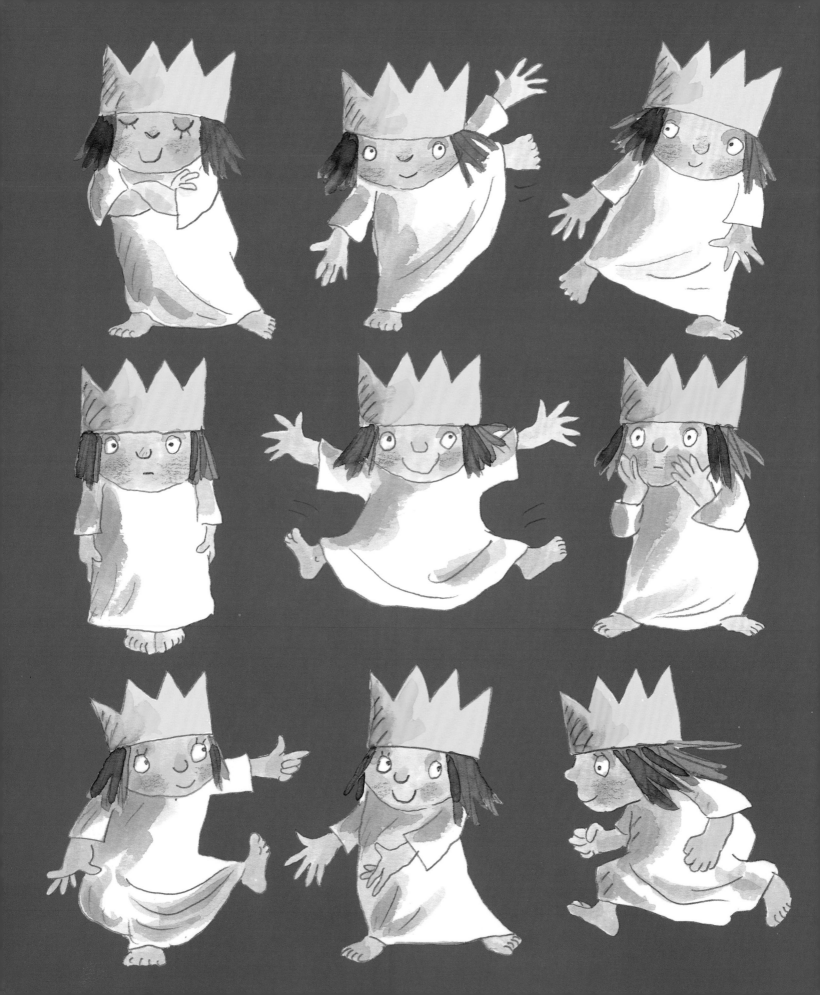

This paperback edition first published in 2009 by Andersen Press Ltd.

First published in Great Britain in 2006 by Andersen Press Ltd.,

20 Vauxhall Bridge Road, London SW1V 2SA.

Published in Australia by Random House Australia Pty.,

Level 3, 100 Pacific Highway, North Sydney, NSW 2060.

Copyright © Tony Ross, 2006.

The rights of Tony Ross to be identified as the author and illustrator of this work have

been asserted by him in accordance with the Copyright, Designs and Patents Act, 1988.

All rights reserved. Colour separated in Switzerland by Photolitho AG, Zürich.

Printed and bound in China by Foshan Zhao Rong Printing Co., Ltd.

10   9   8   7   6   5   4   3   2   1

British Library Cataloguing in Publication Data available.

ISBN 978 1 84270 715 9 (Trade paperback edition)

ISBN 978 1 78344 027 6 (Riverside edition)

A Little Princess Story

I Want to Go Home!

Tony Ross

Andersen Press

One day, the Queen found a new castle.

"This one's too small, now we have your brother!"

"And then, there's that lot," she said.

"And THAT LOT . . ."
"I don't want to live somewhere else,"
said the Little Princess.

"Oh, yes you do," said the Queen.
"You'll have much more room."

So, the Duke of Somewhereorother
bought the old castle . . .

. . . and the Little Princess moved into the new one.

"I WANT TO GO HOME!" said the Little Princess.

"You ARE home," said the Queen. "Look at your posh new room. It's big, and full of your things."

"I WANT TO GO HOME!" said the Little Princess.

"But look at the new garden," said the Queen.
"Perhaps the Gardener will let you help him."

"I WANT TO GO HOME!" said the Little Princess.

"But look at the new kitchen," said the Queen.
"I want to go home NOW!" said the Little Princess.

"Very well," said the Queen. "You can go back
to the old castle, but only for a peep."

"The Duke of Somewhereorother lives
there now. Look, he's painted it!"

"The Dukelet lives in your old room!"

"Look at the lovely new kitchen!"
said the Duchess of Somewhereorother.

"And see how nice the garden is
without those horrible trees . . ."

"We could have tea and cake on the lawn . . .

. . . so long as you don't drop crumbs."

"After all, we don't want birds, do we? I have
to hoover the grass every day as it is."

"I WANT TO GO HOME!" said the Little Princess.
"ME TOO!" said the Queen.

"Mmmmmmmmm!" said the Little Princess.
"This is more like it!"

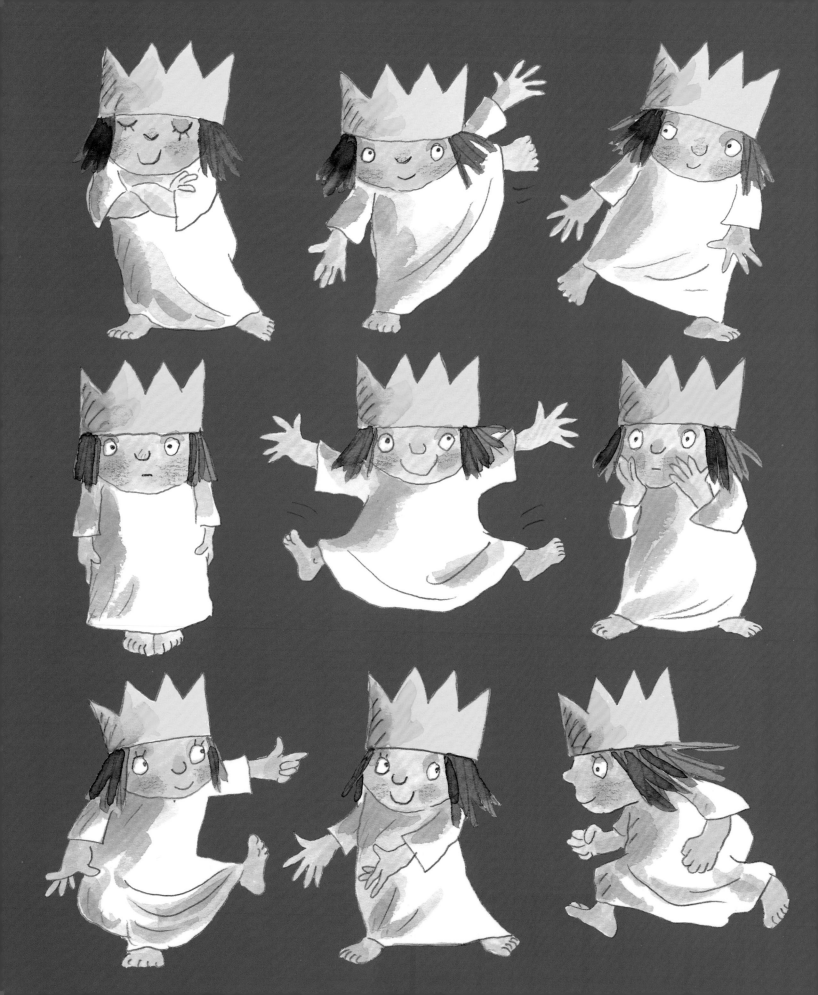

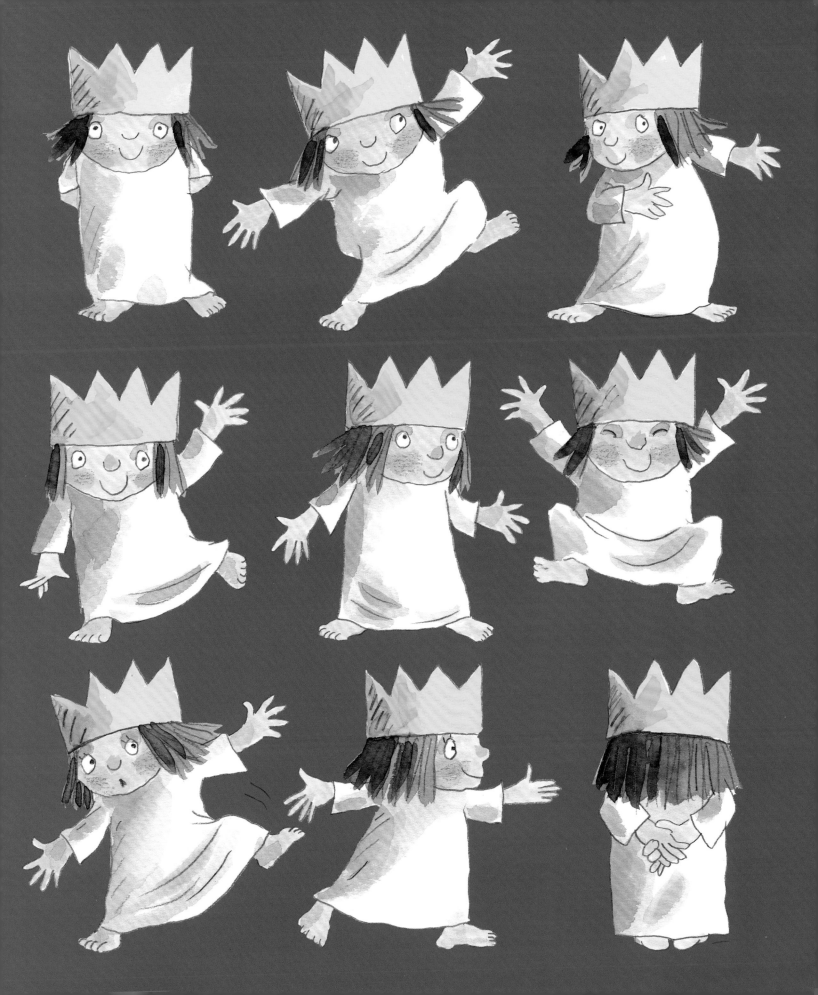

Other Little Princess Books

I Didn't Do it!

I Don't Want to Go to Hospital!

I Don't Want to Wash My Hands!

I Want a Boyfriend!

I Want a Party!

I Want a Sister!

I Want My Dummy!

I Want My Light On!

I Want My Potty!

I Want to Be!

I Want to Do it By Myself!

I Want to Go Home!

I Want to Win!

I Want Two Birthdays!

Little Princess titles are also available as eBooks.

LITTLE PRINCESS TV TIE-INS

Fun in the Sun!

I Want to Do Magic!

I Want My Sledge!

I Don't Like Salad!

I Don't Want to Comb My Hair!

I Want to Go to the Fair!

I Want to Be a Cavegirl!

I Want to Be Tall!

I Want My Sledge! Book and DVD